T0077962

APORIA
Lament of an Ambazonian Revolutionary

Peter Wuteh Vakunta

Langaa Research & Publishing CIG
Mankon, Bamenda

Publisher:

Langaa RPCIG
Langaa Research & Publishing Common Initiative Group
P.O. Box 902 Mankon
Bamenda
North West Region
Cameroon
Langaagrp@gmail.com
www.langaa-rpcig.net

Distributed in and outside N. America by African Books Collective
orders@africanbookscollective.com
www.africanbookscollective.com

ISBN-10: 9956-551-56-2

ISBN-13: 978-9956-551-56-9

Dedication

To all fallen soldiers of the Ambazonian Revolution

Acknowledgement

Special thanks go to my friends in academia who read this work and made pertinent comments that led to the final product.

Aporia: Lament of an Ambazonian Revolutionary is a long poem that speaks to all and sundry—Ambazonians at home and in the diaspora, sympathizers to the cause of Southern Cameroonians on the African continent and on the global scene. This book is a lampoon of the ongoing genocide in Cameroon. It is my conviction that the task of the genuine intellectual is to speak up when no one dares to speak. Throughout life, from the cradle to the grave, we store up information culled from lived experiences; from the travails of others, and try in some laborious fashion to make sense of it all. When we draw a blank and cannot make sense of the events that have deeply perturbed our lives, we have recourse to the plume in a bid to externalize pent-up emotions. Poetry is one of the channels through which I externalize my thoughts. Versification is arguably a passionate art form. It provides me with an outlet for exploring innermost thoughts and emotions. Poetry allows me to communicate issues that I would otherwise sweep under the carpet. It affords me the opportunity to re-evaluate myself, my relationship with others, my station in life, and the world around me. Poetry can be therapeutic, allowing us to wade through turbulences in our lives in quest of solutions, clarity, comfort, and peace of mind. It provides a vehicle of the expression of conflictual attitudes and insights.

The impetus to write *Aporia: Lament of an Ambazonian Revolutionary* came from the genocide that is ongoing in Cameroon; a civil war viewed by many domestic and international role-players as a by-product of dysfunctional governance, lethal tribalism, shameless kleptomania and deleterious governmental ineptitude in the body politic of that country. Each verse in this poem is the voice of the poet; a piece of his mind that yearns to bring sanity to an insane world.

"No race can prosper till it learns that there is as much dignity in tilling a field as in writing a poem."

[**Booker T. Washington**]

When did the rains
Start to fall on Ambazonians?
Where did the dark rain clouds gather?
Was it in Foumban
Or at Ntarikon Park?
When did the palapala begin?
Who lit the fire of conflagration?
Was it the Teachers' Trade Union
Or the Lawyers' Association?
Who organized it?
Was it Deacon Wilfred Tassang
Or Mancho Bibixy?
There are founding fathers.
Who are they?
Fon Gorgi Dinka,
Carlson Anyangwe,
Simon Munzu,
Albert Womah Mukong…
Who formed the Interim Government (IG)?
Was it Sisiku Julius Ayuk Tabe
Or Deacon Wilfred Tassang?
Where does Agbor Felix Balla Nkongho
Stand in all that has transpired?
Take a pulse of the Revolution—
Moving TGV (Train à Grande Vitesse)
Or sinking Titanic in dire need of S.O.S?
Man no run!
Man no die man rotten!
In this day and age,
Who heads the Revolution?
Samuel Ikome Sako or Christopher Anu?
Or is it Ayaba Cho Lucas?
What does the acronym SOCADEF stand for?

1

Southern Cameroons Defense Force!
Who is the Commander-in-Chief of SOCADEF?
Is it Ayaba Cho Lucas or
Ebenezer Derek Mbongo Akwanga?
What other sheep constitute the flock?
Eric Tataw,
Elvis Kometa,
Mark Bareta,
Ntonfuon Boh Hebert,
Ivo Tapang,
Dabney Yerima,
John Mbah Akuro,
Fontem Neba…
Are these wolves in sheep's skin?
Alternatively, bona fide liberators?
The litmus test of time will tell.
When a people grope around
In pitch darkness
Oblivious of who they are
Begging to know where they are going
Maybe that is because
They do not know
Where they hail from
And if they know not
Their provenance
Then they have failed in the quest
For the fundamental self
Maybe that is because
They are out of touch with reality
A rediscovery of the ordinary
Oftentimes,
We have been branded
Beasts of no nation

The lost generation of Ambasonia
Aliens in the land of our birth
Some have christened
The children of this Amba Land/
Alias Federal Republic of Ambazonia
Cum Southern Cameroons,
Food for military canon
Of the LRC junta,
Maybe that's because
The future holds no good
No light at the end of the tunnel
For the *jeunes talents*[1]
Of this blighted nation
Caught in the crossfire
And telltale demagoguery
Of political *djintété*[2]
Utterly swamped by the
Hullabaloo of tribalism
And the brouhaha of ethnic cleansing
Tribal emasculation,
Swayed by the whirlwind
Of cronyism and cult worship.
No gainsaying the fact that
When the *grands katikas*[3] do battle
The *tchotchoros*[4] of Ambazonia

---

[1] Young children

[2] Bigshot

[3] From the English word "care-taker". The word refers to a security guard in charge of a public place like a cinema, recreation ground, casino, etc. It entered Cameroon Pidgin English in the late 1980s among urban dwellers, as expressed essentially in oral discourse.

[4] Little children. Speakers of Cameroon Pidgin English have used this word since 1980s.

Leak their gaping wounds.
Smothering discontent
May lurk around like the *nyamangoro*[5]/
However, there comes a time
When even the *mbutuku*[6]
Picks up their boxing gloves
Like Mohammed Ali,
Like ear-munching Mike Tyson
And enters the infernal Ring/
To do battle with the foe
Until death do them part,
Rather than pick *tokyo*[7]
And run *nine-ninety*[8] like an *opep*[9]
Hotly pursued by *mange-mille*[10]
Die man no de fia bury grong![11]
So it came to pass
In that fateful year 1990
When the *kanas*[12] man of Ntarikon
Ni John Fru Ndi
Our Latter Day Moses
Bit the bullet and set

---

[5] Literally "snail" and by extension, a slow, nonchalant person or trivial affair.

[6] Abbreviated from the word "mbutuku", which means "a good-for-nothing person, "a weakling" or "an idiot". Mainly used by young people, this loanword exists in Cameroon Pidgin English since the 1970s.

[7] Run

[8] Fast

[9] Illegally operated taxi.

[10] [10] The lowest ranking member of the police force, unbeatable when it comes to extorting money from taxi drivers on the streets. Literally, it means "eat-a-thousand".

[11] A dead man is not scared of the cemetery

[12] Male genitals, testicles; courage

The macabre ball rolling
Rolling and rolling nonstop!
The advent of the SDF:
Social Democratic Front
Amid much pomp and fanfare
Was a storm in the teacup
Political formation that has
Ere long remained
The albatross of Mbiya Mbivodo
Absentee tenant at Etoudi,
Roi fainéant ruling a land
He has no clue what it is all about.
Came fire/ came brimstone
Came rain/came sun/came thunder
The aftermath was ravaging
Numerous sons- of- the- soil
And daughters- of- the- soil
Cut down in their prime of youth
Purportedly crushed in a stampede
Myriads gave up the ghost in a bloodbath
That left all and sundry dumfounded
The truth of the matter is your guess
It is mine too
Several of my *tara*[13]/
Picked up from *matango*[14] houses
From *matutu*[15] taverns
And mbu houses,
And from swine quarter
And much to their dismay,

---

[13] Friends
[14] Palm-wine
[15] Raffia wine

Were thrown into *ngata*[16].
Some found themselves at BMM Up station
The *Tisong*[17] *Brigade Mixte Mobile*[18]
Manned by satanic motherfuckers,
Notorious for its atheistic credo
Dieu est Mort: God is Dead!
None was a *sansanboy*[19]
Not one was an *opposant*[20]
Sexually starved soldiers
Raped my *mini-minor*[21] sisters
At Ngoa Ekelle in broad day light.
Hundreds more pounded/
Like *poto-poto by unlettered zangalewa*[22],
Lay rotting in mass graves to date!
Their ghosts ignited
The infamous *villes mortes*
Infamous ghost-town operations
That brought economic life
To a virtual standstill
In Mimboland/
And became anathema to
Wheezy-voiced dumbass President
De la Répulique ongolaise.
Taximen and *bayam-sellam*[23]

---

[16] Prison

[17] Bamenda

[18] Mixed Mobile Brigade

[19] Smart boy, rascal

[20] Member of an opposition political party.

[21] Refers to a young woman who has not yet attained puberty. In some contexts, it may refer to a young prostitute.

[22] Mud; or something valueless. The presence of this word in Cameroonian French dates from the 1940s.

[23] Market women

Unsung heroes of No Man's Land
Doggedly refused to throw in the towel
The *Takumbeng*[24]
Symbol of feminine steel
Joined the processional dirge
Baying for Mbivodo's blood
Chanting with alacrity—
Barlok for youa head, Mbivodo![25]
Na helele-o!
Trobu for youa pikin dem head, Mbiya![26]
Na helele-o! Na helele-o!
Woman power na las[27] *power!*
Na helele-o! Na helele-o!
Tell we say no be woman born you![28]
Na helele-o! Na helele-o!
Tell we say na mboma born you![29]
Na helele-o! Na helele-o!
Bereaved families consulted
Maguida[30] for *gris-gris*[31]
Many more went to seek fortification
From the *mami-wata*[32]
Water spirits
Of Lake Oku
Of Lake Manenguba

---

[24] Group of elderly women participating in a protest
[25] We wish you bad luck!
[26] Woe unto to your children
[27] Vagina
[28] Tell us that you are not born of a woman
[29] Tell us that your mother is a boa constrictor
[30] Muslim from one of the Northern regions in Cameroon
[31] Amulets
[32] Female water spirits who, from time to time, come to torment men.

7

Of Lake Menchum
And of Lake Nyos
And of Lake Barombi
Aquatic inhabitants
Of the Sanaga River
And of the Mungo River
The intent:
Smoke Mbivodo
And his Ali Baba Gang
Out of his hideout at Etoudi
The People's Shithouse
Den of compulsive chop-broke-potters!
Sons of a bitch!
Good for nothing jackasses!
Spendthrift pussies!
Betis are Ongola's anathema,
They are Locusts
Hell-bent on crippling the nation
By having recourse to
Necromancy and megalomania
Through democraZy and kleptomania
Locusts/
These nefarious insects don't build
They destroy/They dilapidate!
Crogg/ crogg/ crogg/
They've destroyed our economies/
They've destroyed our coffee plants.
Locusts/
Cragg/ cragg/ cragg/
Bastards! Assholes!
Emasculators of social justice!
These hoodlums don't nurture/
They devastate with impunity!

They've destroyed our industries
Produce Marketing Board/
Sonara Limbe,
Ndu Tea,
Tole Tea,
Socapalm,
Cameroon Development Corporation,
Cameroon Bank,
Mideno and Midevef,
Upper Nun Valley Development Authority,
Crugg/crugg/crugg,
Indolent nitwits!
They are Locusts!
Makanana! Makanana!
Nation's gravediggers!
They have destroyed our livelihood,
They have destroyed our palm trees,
They have destroyed our cocoa plantations,
They have destroyed our banana plantations,
They have dilapidated our forests,
They have dilapidated our sources of income.
Crigg/crigg/crigg
Locusts,
These insects are hard
At work destroying
The legacy bequeathed
To Us by Forebears
Locusts are in charge of
Our collective destiny
Shall they make or mar?
That is the question!
It's time for fumigation!
In Abakwa,

The downtrodden chanted:
Mbiya is really something!
He must go!
Facing Mount Cameroon,
Chariot of the gods,
The wretched of the earth roared,
Red card for Mbivodo!
In Bafoussam and Bafang,
In Loum Chantiers Gare,
In Penja and Dibombari,
In Nkongsamba and Kake,
Irate rioters sang freedoms songs—
Liberté eh, eh!
Liberté eh eh eh eh !
Dieu tout puissant ah ah!
Nous serons libres bientôt![33]
In Nkambe and Wum,
In Bamunka and Babessi,
In Bamali and Babungo,
In Bambili and Bambui,
In Bali and Babanki,
Disillusioned protesters chorused:
Liberty, eh, eh!
Liberty eh, eh, eh, eh!
All-powerful God, ah ah!
Soon we will be free!
We shall overcome-eh eh!
The gods of our ancestors
Are in full control-ooh!
But the Man,

---

[33] Quoted in Patrice Nganang's Temps de chien published by Le serpent à plumes, 2001.

Being no spring chicken/
Smelling *arata*[34]/ he sneaked incognito
Into the equatorial forest,
To obtain from his pygmy tribesmen/
Megan[35] which he carried on his person
Day in day out / night and day/
As backup for his European-tailored/
Bullet-proof jacket/
In his peregrinations/
Journeys through the ghost nation/
GHOST TOWNS OPERATIONS…
Towns haunted by ghosts of victims!
The ghost of Eric Takou,
Phantoms of freedom fighters,
Corpses of fallen heroes,
Cut down by bullets fired by
Trigger-happy soldiers and *gendarmes*[36]
Haunted the land in perpetuity
The brutal killing of innocent kids
Shocked women who exposed their vaginas
To the killers protesting the
Murder of innocent victims
The corpse of Takou
Paraded in a *pousse-pousse*[37]
By incensed inhabitants of Douala
Later deposited at the doorstep of his assassin.
VENDETTA…
First it had been students,

---

[34] Rat
[35] Witchcraft
[36] Police officer in francophone Africa
[37] Wheel-cart

Then came civil servants,
Now the black marketers
Joined the macabre dance,
Refusing to be subdued by municipal vampires.
They stood firm in the face of imminent danger
Then came the turn of taxi drivers
Who refused to commute,
Protesting the legal shakedowns by the police.
They mourned colleagues
Shot at point-blank range
By sycophantic *mbere khaki*[38]
Then came the turn of *bendskin*[39] drivers;
The frogs call them *bendskinneurs,*
Who took to the streets of New Bell,
To protest the brutal killing of one
Of theirs murdered by a *mange-mille* on duty
The deceased had refused to *tchoko*[40]
As mandated by jungle justice
In that hellhole called Ongola.
Commuters had gone on strike
To protest this endemic human cruelty.
The day they went on strike
All streets were emptied of its human cargo,
From time to time,
A helicopter would cross the sky
Men hid in *boutiques*[41]
And off-licence bars,
Alias vente à emporter.

---

[38] Policemen
[39] Motor-bike taxi drivers
[40] Give a bribe
[41] Shops

Purporting that the
Helicopters carried lethal tear-gas
And machine-guns
Grenades/and bombs!
Harbinger of the arrival of
The much dreaded alien mermaids—
MAMI WATA…
Theirs is the tale of a time
When humans no longer have the time
To think creatively
There is decadence,
There is depravity,
There is *je m'enfoutisme*[42]
We live in a world
Characterized by impunity.
Dog-eat-dog paradise!
There is angst in high gear,
Roads and streets
Bespattered with excrement.
There is craziness,
There is wanton abuse,
Married men keep *deuxième bureaux*[43]/
Housewives keep sugar daddies/
Some call them blessed and blessers
Peu importe! It boils down to la même chose!
Common sense has become nonsense,
Good food has become poison,
Deleterious to the human body.
It engenders a surfeit of flesh,
That hurts the public eye.

---

[42] Attitude of I couldn't care less
[43] Mistresses

I left my motherland in order
To know the world better.
However, the more I learn about humanity,
The more I get befuddled!
The more ignorant I become.
There is time to learn,
And time to teach.
There is time to be lost,
And time to find one's way.
Time to chase shadows,
And time to return to one's roots.
I am black and proud,
Even the sun would testify.
Exile has made me lose my bearings.
As time ages,
I realize I have fallen into decadence,
Like the sleepwalker,
Groping around in the thick fog of myopia,
Eyes wide open,
I have become a *mami-wata*.
I take a look around me,
And I ape others/
Like a cultural bastard!
Bastardy everywhere!
Bastardization of languages!
Emasculation of cultures!
Because we believe their fate is rosier,
We believe they have a better understanding
Of universalism,
Of social engineering,
Of the summum bonum,
Of political correctness,
And of how to be and not to be,

Of what's fair and what is unfair.
We believe they know
How far they want to go,
And when to stop,
When to forge ahead and when to retreat.
Alas, it has dawned on me that,
Other cultures are not aborted attempts
At being my own culture;
Other races are not miscarriages
Of my own race,
They are unique manifestations
Of Divine ingenuity and artisanship.
The world in which I live
Is only one model of human reality
I do not know
When I became the Other.
What I do know is that
I straighten out my hair
With maximum-strength hair products.
I do not know
When I became the alter ego.
What I do know is that:
I do flake my skin with Venus de Milo
I brutalize my body in order to minimize it.
I do not have breasts
My buttocks are flat,
Like the surface of the earth.
I am as tiny as a blade of elephant grass
In the Grassfields of Bamenda,
Such Eves are labeled Akwara!
In Mimboland, they're called Wolowoss
It is a question of necessity,
I have to please the mundane world

I look like a breadboard,
Therefore, I am pretty.
I dance in circles on chilly nights,
Men in hot pants vie
With one another in admiration
Of my battered anatomy.
When I walk around my dry bones crackle,
On the left then on the right,
Causing cocky men to wink,
In addition, salivate in their sagging pants!
In addition, work up an erotic sweat!
Masturbation! Ejaculation!
I savor this sleazy victory,
While cleaning public lavatories for a pittance,
Miles away from home in the diaspora,
I know them all—
I could give you a description
Of all types of men who come here—
There are handsome old men,
Who would tell you that they'd teach you,
How to sleep with a woman,
They will tell you that they will teach you
The act and the art of lovemaking,
These scallywags have no clue
What the world has become
In spite of them, you know!
Alas, you would not understand a damned thing,
Because before they're done teaching you,
You would find them stretched out on you,
As if in a suicidal attempt
To escape from the ravages of time.
There are the fat ones who stop thinking
About their monstrous bodies

When they smell the odor of sex,
Of vapor exuding from excrement and urine
In the unkempt loos and lavatories.
They say they will teach you silent generosity,
By offering you the rare opportunity
To take a peep at their greasy balls.
Then there are women with anthill breasts.
There are those with breasts
As flat as a pair of *sans confiance*[44]
Rich and poor who give the impression
That they have the umbilical cord
Of the universe between their thighs
Elles se croient sorties de la cuisse de Jupiter
As the Gaulois would have it.
They would not say a word to you,
As if by some mystery you have come
To share their station in life,
Darned assholes! Nitwits!
In addition, that is EVEN better!
I do not know when
I became a ghost of myself.
It does happen
When people live
In close proximity to one another,
When days go by in great at terrific speed,
And become weeks and turn into months,
And months metamorphose into years.
One day the weather is awesome.
The next day it is awful,
And we're WHITE women
And we BLACK men

---

[44] Cheap slippers made out of rubber.

I am certainly not European
I look into the mirror
Day in day out
And I know for sure
That I am not European—

Look at my lips;
Look at my nose;
Look at my hair;
Look at my skin;
I am not a European
But of course
This hardly precludes
The possibility of a
Meaningful DIALOGUE
With the TOUBAB[45]
There could be *brassage des races*
Of the White and the Black
In winter,
In summer,
In autumn,
In spring,
In the rainy season,
In the dry season,
We dance attendance to,
The dictates of colorism,
We dare not take our eyes off the ground,
Lest we falter and fall on social scum,
Lying pell-mell on the sidewalk,
If I'd taken my eyes off the tarmac,
From time to time intermittently,

---

[45] White man

Just at the right moment,
It would have dawned on me,
That sometimes there is light in the clouds,
At times, there is darkness in the sun,
Times have changed,
Much is still to come.
The future alone should matter,
Even the *nyam fuka*[46] knows that!
BEASTS OF NO NATION…
For the sake of the future indeed,
We PUMP up inside gym-clubs,
Our beauty wilts in sauna baths,
We crush tons of fat
Because we need bare bones.
We will look attractive to lascivious men,
Like dogs they rave and rant,
Nose up in the air they chuckle.
When one of them manages
To get hold of one of us,
He shows off with her puny body
At wife-swapping parties
He would say tongue in cheek:
Have you met my sweetheart?
A real model!
He whispers into her ear
Laughing up his sleeve
Excited and contented
We ARE *mami-wata*
CASTERS of spells
We intoxicate men with potions

---

[46] Beasts

We charm them with *tobassi*[47]
TOBASSI…
How many times have I seen men
Send their toe under the table in matango[48] clubs
In the space between the legs
Of their neighbor's woman
And even take the lid off her *garde-manger*[49]
We intoxicate our men with *megan*[50]
We are heroes of sorts.
FALLEN HEROES
Hail Bate Besong!…
He's not here
Yet far and away
Echoes of his prolific
Erudition resounds
BB's not here
But the legacy of his
Intellect lives here
He is not here
But rumblings of his
Vociferous castigation
Of an inept system clamors
He's is not here
Still everywhere
The melody of his lampoon
Against a cantankerous polity chimes
Hail Obasinjom Warrior!
The genuine intellectual

---

[47] Charm
[48] Palm-wine
[49] Private parts
[50] Witchcraft

The man who relegated
Pseudo-intellectualism
To the trashcan of academia
BB is no more
Long live Bate Besong!
Long live the immortal!
The wonder boy of Akwaya
Big or small
Rich or poor
Corruptible or incorruptible
Miscreant or holier-than-thou
BB, Chums with Bole Butake
Whose brainchild is *Lake God*
You sure are familiar
With this gadfly of the Makanana Regime,
The wonder boy from Donga Mantung
Or is it Bui Division?
Peu importe! Doesn't matter!
Heroes go and heroes come,
Writers don't die; they transition,
From dust we came
Unto dust we will return
We will all die
We do so singly
Not even kings
Will be accompanied
On their extra-terrestrial journey
By a convoy of pages.
Hail Reuben Um Nyobé!
Bête noire of Gaullist Africa
Enfant terrible[51] of Ahidjoic regime

---

[51] Black sheep

Maquisard of Sanaga Maritime
Die-hard Upeciste
Like a beast of burden he wandered
Hither and thither
In the heart of the Sanaga Forest
Unfazed by fear of the unknown
Feeding on roots and branches
Oblivious to birds of ill omen
Communing with birds of good omen
He elected domicile
On the banks of the Sanaga River
Eating raw fish and cassava tubers
He gallivanted in the deep of night
Tiptoeing in and out of hideouts
Walking in the burning bushes
Alert to sounds of goodwill
As they whispered to him good tidings
BAOBAB!
He was a Lion-Man
Man with a heart of steel
Man with the tongue of fire
Man born before his age
He knew the nooks and crannies of
French conspiratorial machinations—
The ultimate declaration of love-hate
For the arch-enemy
UNSUNG HERO
Hail Albert Womah Mukong!
The unfazed diehard
Babanki Tungo
Pet peeve of Africa's colonialists

Ennemi numéro un[52] of inept regimes
At daggers drawn with half-book
President Ahmdou Ahidjo.
Recidivist inmate of Mantoun prison
Prisoner without a crime
Graduate of Kondengui
Maximum-security dungeon,
Located in Yaoundé,
The eyesore capital of Mimboland
Hail Ernest Ouandié!
Object of public opprobrium
Sacrificial lamb of political thuggery
Ashes of freedom
Flesh of flesh/Bone of bone/
Like the Iroko tree, you refused to be bent
Like the mahogany tree
You refused to let your arm be twisted,
To be daunted by combat
The baobab tree lent you its shade
In the Sanaga swamps
The equatorial jungle your abode
Your companion in battle
It was said to you:
The revolution was made without YOU!
Your own tribesmen disowned YOU!
To the utter dismay of roaming hyenas
Was there a crisis of identity?
IDENTITY CRISIS…
Je ne sais pas au juste qui je suis
I do not quite know who I am
D'autres m'appellent Froggie

---

[52] Enemy number one

Some call me Anglo
Je ne sais toujours pas qui je suis
I still do not know who I am
My name is Le Bamenda
Mon nom c'est Enemy in the house
L'Ennemi dans la maison
My name c'est le Biafrais
Mon nom is underclass citizen
Clumsy citizen from Ambaland.
My name c'est le maladroit
Taisez-vous! Shut up!
Do not bother me!
Ne m'embêtez pas!
Don't you know that
Je suis ici chez moi?
Vous ignorez que
I belong here?
I shall fight to my dernier souffle
To forge a real name pour moi-même
You shall call me Anglo-frog!
Vous m'appellerez Franglo!
Shut up! Taisez-vous!
Do not bother me!
Ne m'embêtez pas!
Vous ignorez que I belong here?
Don't you know that
Je suis ici chez moi?
I shall fight to my last breath
To forge a real lingo for myself
I will speak Français
Je parlerai English
Together we will speak camfranglais
C'est-à-dire qu'ensemble

We will speak le Camerounisme
Because here nous sommes
Tous chez nous! I di tell wuna !
A bon entendeur salut!
He who has ears should hear!
Hear the macabre dance
BREAK DANCE AT BAKASSI…
In Longkak
Tchoum/Tchoum!
Sing the Ntarikonic requiem of zombification
Tchoum/Tchoumassa
Tchoumassa of disembowelers
Tchoumassa of defilers of teenagers
Of scavengers of graveyards in Muyuka!
Of assassins of school kids in Ngoketunjia!
At the *Marché* Mokolo[53]/
Tchoum/Tchoumassa
Dirge for rappers of Amba girls in Bamenda
And Buea, Kumba and Mutengene
Tchoum/Tchoum!
Tchoumassa of vampires
In Bafut and Bali Nyonga
Tchoum/Tchoum!
Takumbeng Dance for the demise
Of elements of BIR in Ambasonia.
One/ two/three/four!
Stamp your flat feet
Sing Tchoumassa of putrefaction
Grab your *mami-wata merengue*
Partner by the waist in honor of John.
The *chaud gars* of Tisong!

---

[53] Mokolo Market

Turn her around to face the hearth fire
Tchoum/Tchoum/Tchoumassa
Credo of *alikamouti*[54]
Consumer of tender flesh
Regurgitating the entrails of victims
Of poisoned gifts
Of sacrificial lambs
Tchoum/Tchoumassa
Credo of men of the underworld
Of coupeur *de route*[55]
Of high-way robbers
Hounded by forces of law and order
In love with Dan *sapak*[56]/
WOLOWOSS[57]
GALORE!
Looking at these images
Your gait and your demeanor speak volumes/
Young girl / mini-skirt wearer
Ere long deflowered by famished predators
Young woman/wearing revealing dress
Skillful hunters of men
Tell-tales tattoos speak
Volumes about your lot in life
Heart-broken I am/ looking at these portraits
OF YOU AND OF ILK
And you sista[58] of Ntamulung Quarter
Reduced to carnal trade to earn a living
Nothing more to say

---

[54] Vampire
[55] Highway robber
[56] Prostitute
[57] Whore
[58] Sister

AND YOU
Scallywag!
Scavenger of street scum
Hands sullied with social grime
Crime of nepotism
Opium of the people
AND YOU
Prison graduate in cell Number Zero
Prisoner with trumped charges/
Crucified on the cross of witch-hunt
Aided and abetted by the credo of
La politique du ventre[59]
THE POET
Writes wants he wants,
I will write what I want.
To write or not to write
To be or to be not
That is the question!
Fornicator of ideas
Fumigator of illusions
Of self-delusion
Virtuoso of craftsmanship
Experts at cooking the books!
Heir of a nation in the pipeline
ME!
I write poetry
Therefore I am
Herald of ill-wind/
Purveyor of discomfiture
To speak or not to speak
Dilemma of the griot

---

[59] Belly politics

THE BARD

Voice of the voiceless
Loquacious peace-lover
Taciturn talkative
YOU…
Garrulous pen pusher,
You create your own world
A world of intoxication
YOU… ME…TOWN CRIERS…
 We…whistle-blowers…
We create worlds
Devoid of PREVARICATION
Man and ilk are locking horns in
Infectious mutual suspicion in
The Ambazonian Revolution---
Successful revolutions are
Are engineered by politically savvy
And bona fide intellectuals;
Not hoodlums, conmen and scumbags.
Many of us in this struggle
Are under the influence of the latter.
Surely, it should not be beyond
The wit of Ambazonians,
Most of us bred and nurtured
In elite institutions such as
Sacred Heart College (my Alma Mater),
CPC Bali, Our Lady of Lourdes, SASSE
And more to devise a paradigm
That circumvents deleterious
And counterproductive discourses.
This I say irrespective of
Whether there is a communal pact
Between brokers in the Revolution.

It cannot be that any party seeks
To force a pact by violent,
Self-destructive Modus operandi.
Even if such a pact were possible,
It would not be worth the paper
On which it has been written,
For behind such a pact,
There will be no mutual understanding.
What is worse, even after
A pact is arrived at there would
Be so much to expect that
There would never be any
Communal plan of action
Poet and man of law, I have
Dedicated myself to uphold the law.
Poet and man of law, I fully
Embrace the principle that each of us
Is subject to the law;
That each of us is BOUND to obey
The law enacted by governments and
Institutionalized social contracts.
Nonetheless, if I lived in Nazi Germany,
I believe I would have refused to
Wear an armband to hail Hitler!
How can I reconcile my profound
Adherence to legality and accountability
With bashful and iniquitous comportment
Within the Ambazonian Revolution?
Is there a principle, a code of conduct,
Or a theory to which a man with honor
And integrity may subscribe?
Or is it just a matter of Machiavellian impulses?

Do we live in a trackless jungle?
Or in an ontological maze?
Where do we situate the
Ambazonian Revolution alias
The Southern Cameroonian Dilemma
In this scheme of affairs?
In this veritable conundrum?
Is there or is there not a path
That law and integrity mark out
Through the maze of our tangled
Obligations to the departed souls on GZ?
Above all, it is critical for us
To know whether or not
Impunity and lawlessness
Are effective alternatives.
I lay my case here and revert
To the bunker where
Wife thinks husband is lying
Husband believes wife is cheating
Child thinks parent is fibbing
Parent thinks child is faking
Tax collector believes
Taxpayer is fawning
Taxpayer thinks
Tax collector is feigning
The politician thinks
The electorate is acting up
Voters think candidates
Are wheeling and dealing
Pretty load of hogwash!
Garbed in multifaceted masks
We make believe in all walks of life—
Conmen pass for liberators,

Servants of Satan simulate Pastors
Foes act like friends
Friends ape foes
This world's theater for Apemania!
Mortals impersonate immortals
Humans pass for super humans
Miscreants act the pious
Self-seekers masquerade
As selfless philanthropists
The world is like a mask
He that desires to see well
Dare not stand in one spot
The Muses said this would happen:
That Revolution would be hijacked
And words will be twisted out of signification
By a couple of tricksters,
Scallywags and daredevils!
From the Tower of Double-Speak,
To the pits of Ground Zero,
And from thence we will live in Infernal Babel
At daggers drawn baying for each other's blood!
Words would get crooked
And more and more doctored
As meaning is slaughtered
At the Alter of linguistic jugglery
Until no one would understand
What the other is saying
Tower of Babel! Inferno!
Or to look at the mouth
Of his neighbor
When it is best to shut up!
Fermez-la! Espèce d'ignares!
We live in that time

That the Sage had predicted
Nothing means what is said
What is said is not what is heard!
Putain! Sale Putain!
And what is done is not what is said,
Words say what they do not mean to say,
In our pseudo lingo,
SLANGUAGE…
Penchant for convoluted syllables
Notoriety to make the ordinary
Sound extraordinary.
Parliamentarians have become
The peoples' Choke-holders!
Heads of State have become
 Pirates of the Nation!
Our chiefs have metamorphosed into leeches.
Our Fons have become Fons without Fondoms.
Academics enjoy the rare privilege of being
Branded roving libraries
The mentally retarded
Are intellectually challenged
Elevator operators pass for
Vertical transportation corps
Double-speak/
Our stock-in-trade! /
Pre-emptive counter-attack
Veils our penchant for belligerence/
Tactical redeployment/
Euphemism for military retreat/.
We adore circumlocution
Talking crooked in a bid to save face.
We talk from both sides of our mouths!
Trêve de conneries! Salopards!

Convolution being our forte
We no longer have bullet holes
They are ballistic induced apertures
In the subcutaneous environment
Our neutron bombs
Have metamorphosed into
Radiation enhancement contraptions.
We brand COVID-19 Chinese Virus!
Incriminating news dismissed as Fake News!
Yeah! We freaking smart you know?
We have the gall to play God!
Double-speak breeds verbal fire
I barely comprehend what I they say
What I desire
I speak words
That I do not know
Shit about, seriously!
Where are we going?
We are in the wilderness
Confused by signs
Befuddled by significations
We are in a fast train
Where stoplights are needed
To halt the insanity
We are in a top-speed metro
Where we need signs
To stop the indulgence.
We are in a breakneck train
Where traffic lights are needed
To halt the dementia
We are in a maddening train
Where we need road signs
To put an end to madness.

We are in a high-speed train
Where yellow lights are needed
To halt the derangement
Musings of the poet…
The POET…
Creates a fluid world
Aquatic world
WATER
Water! Water! Everywhere
But not a drop to drink in Ambazonia
Water galore
But not a drop to drink in Menchum
Not a drop in Ndop; in Tiko.
Moral drought at home
Moral drought in the Diaspora!
Drought of efficiency
Drought of leadership,
Drought of apt governance.
Deficiency of labor.
Deficiency of foresight.
Of perspicacity,
Penury of health-care,
Dearth of hospital personnel,
Scarcity of town planners,
Hospitals in Baden-Baden ooh!
But not one in Mvomeka'a!
Not one in Yaounde!
Not one in Buea!
Not one in Bamenda!
Poverty in Ebolowa,
Drought of hard cash,
Billions stashed in Swiss banks,
Millions stashed in the ceilings

Of thieving ministers,
And in *Banque de France*[60]
But not a cent in Cameroon Bank.
Gone bankrupt!
Dry season everywhere
Dry season of patriotism
Of self-confidence
Of mutual trust
Of self-esteem
Graffi against Sawa
Some are branded come-no go
In the very Ambaland
We fighting and dying for!
Bassa against Beti,
Drought of camaraderie,
Bangwa against Bali,
Bamileke against Bafaw.
Drought of reciprocal love,
Fulani against Fang,
Banso against Banja,
Drought of barren land
Dryness of non-committal wedlock
Of a forced marriages
In a land awash with the occult
Cult of Famla
Of Essingan
Cult of cannibalistic totemism
Of Maraboutism
Cult of *Ngambe*-houses[61]
Cult of megan houses

---

[60] Bank of France
[61] Witchdoctor sanctuaries

Cult of fetishism.
Of election gerrymandering
DOG-EAT-DOG VENDETTA
In these precincts
Polls are seldom litmus test
Of popular mandate
Benefiting from the privilege
Of incumbency the powers-that-be
Make a sham of fair and free elections
Bashing the precepts of democracy
The legislature transformed
Into a rubberstamp
The judiciary reduced to the posture
Of a toothless bulldog
Barks but seldom bites
Le chien aboie et la caravane passe![62]
The Executive lords it over
A straitjacket Legislature
By fair means and foul
Sins of incumbency
Sins of the flesh
Sins of war
Sins of falsehood
Heinous sins of the Executive
Time for examination of conscience
High time for the intervention of
Qwifon
Of Ngiri
Of Ngumba
Of rainmakers
Rain! Rain! Everywhere

---

[62] The dog barks at the moon

But not a drop in Ngoketunjia.
Not a drop on Mount Fako.
Raindrops of the apocalypse
Raindrops of levity
Raindrops of national decrepitude
Drops of rainwater everywhere
But none for YOU
Water everywhere
But not a drop for ME...
But not a drop for HER...
But not a drop for HIM...
Raindrops of global quarantine,
Raindrops of Armageddon!
Showers of decadence,
Floods of dilapidation,
Dilapidation of the
Deep-water port in Limbe,
Decrepitude the Bamenda
Of the Bamenda Produce Marketing Board
Showers of mock blessing,
Showers of erosion,
Of the Mungo Bridge
Of Palmol in Lobe
Of Socapalm in Dibombari
Showers of auctioneering
At SONARA in Limbe!
Of national banks gone bankrupt
Showers of erosion
Of nationwide plunder
I did not speak
He did!
HE...
Swamp dweller of Elobi/

Tin-shack dweller/
Of Johannesburg
And of Pietersburg/
Sepedi man of Seshego/
Smoking dagga[63] and
Sniffing clue in shacks
Homeless in the land of
High rise buildings/
Setwana speaker/
Of Mpumalanga/
And of Klersdorp/
Dreamless in a land of dreams/
IsiXhosa brother
Of Port Elizabeth/
Penniless in an oasis of plenty/
IsiZulu son of Durban/
And of Pietermaritzburg/
Thirsty in a sea of oceans/
IsiNdebele cousin/
Of Jagersfontein/
Speaker of Fanagalo/
Argot of the diamond mines/
And of the gold mines/
Indigent in the pits of gold mines/
Replete with natural resources/
Teeming with wealth/
Afrikaans speaker/
Of District Six in Cape Town/
Mother City /
Naked indigene of Umtata/
Graduate of Robben Island/

---

[63] Marijuana in Afrikaans

Free born of the Transkei/
Stranger in the land/
Of your own birth/
IsiNdebele fella of Tsonga/
Penny-broke shear-cropper/
Of the Rainbow Nation/
What became of COSATU?
Tsotsitaal speaker/
Of the Northern Cape/
Of Pretoria and Alexandra/
Shame of human of squalor/
Alex! Township in Gauteng Province/
What future have you for your offspring?
Alex, dustbin of Azania[64],
Lies adjacent to posh Suburb of Sandton
Vector of urban misdemeanors
Homeless glue-snuffer
Of the Western Cape
Illiterate in the midst
Of schools and books
Unemployed Xitsonga speaker
Of the Transvaal
Jobless in a land
Replete with jobs
SHE…
I salute HER…
Haggard domestic worker
Of Durban,
The kaffir[65],

---

[64] Original name for South Africa
[65] Insulting name for a black person in South Africa

The Coolie[66],
The Colored[67],
Of the Rainbow Nation.
I hail YOU...
Nanny of Palaborwa
You bend double to
Meet the needs of your bosses
To earn your daily pittance
I salute you…
Au pair of Warm Baths
You toil for your stipend
SiSwati *akwara*[68] of Venda
Sex worker of Soweto
What does the morrow
Hold in store for you?
Yes, there is Soweto
Where many are murdered
In broad day light
For merely asking for the
Right to breathe. Alas!
Yes, there is the wasteland,
Nicknamed Homelands
Where multitudes are fenced in,
Rollicking in abject poverty,
While the masters of the trade
Enjoy exquisite comfort in cities
Tsotsi pickpocket of the townships
Bo-Tsotsi: Youth Gangs of Soweto
Canon for police fodder

---

[66] Unskilled laborer in South Africa, India, China
[67] Person of mixed European and African ancestry in South Africa
[68] Bitch

Sesotho baby-mother
Of Tzaneen
Koi opium cultivator
Of the Kalahari Desert
San Game-hunter
Of Kruger National Park
Uprooted bushman
Of the Namib Desert
And of the Okavango Swamp
Weep not child![69]
My heart bleeds for you!
I weep for all the
Lost souls of Ambazonia!
Strangers in their homeland,
Beasts of no Nation.
I lament for the unborn kids
Of the Republic of Ambazonia
Hijacked kith and kindred.
I mourn for the Six School
Kids murdered in Kumba
Decimated by the vampires of Paul Biya
On October 24, 2020 in the restive
Town of Kumba in a school
Sandwiched in Fiango neighborhood.
The Infamous Mother Francisca
International Bilingual Academy.
We shall never know the real motives behind
This gruesome murder but be it
Known that this infamy was not
The handiwork of Ambazonian
Freedom fighters; rather it was a

---

[69] Title of a novel by Ngugi wa Thiong'o

Machination by the Biya Regime
To baptize Ambazonian Freedom Fighters
As Terrorists. Hogwash! Baloney!
I HAVE A DREAM…
That one day Ambazonia will be free.
Free! Free! Free at last!
From the rubble of decay
And of decrepitude
Will rise a New Nation,
Rejuvenated Republic of Ambazonia!
Not by thunderstorm,
Not by tornado,
Not by hailstone,
Nor by neck-lacing,
Not by house-torching,
Nor by manslaughter,
Not by kangaroo courts
But by the mettle and resolve
Of diehard Ambazonians,
Armed with the resolve to be free.
We are birds of passage
Of good-omen
Of bad omen
Of mixed omens
The good shall not turn into evil
The best be not enemy of the good
Chatter the Doves…
I have half a mind
To turn and live with the birds
They are forever tranquil
And carefree
I watch them in utter admiration
They do not whine about

What they are going to eat the day after
They do not worry about what
The next day holds in store for them
How I wish I were a dove!
Not one of them builds castles in the air
None is victim of inordinate ambition
How I wish I were a dove!
Not one of them abuses power
None lives at the expense of the other
Not even one harbors lustful desires out of season
How I wish I were a dove!
None is like the political chameleon
Changing colors at will
Switching camps at random
For personal gains
I have half a mind
To turn and live with the doves
They all accept their lot in life
LIFE…
My life reads like an open book
Some call it a horror movie
It is pregnant with meaning
Ideas/ words/ feelings/emotions
Hope mingled with despair
Doubts married to certitude
I am a repertoire of knowledge
Granary of cultures/ worldviews
Nursery of self-fulfilling prophesies
I bridge gaps and vacuums/
Mitigating crass ignorance/
I take you around the world/
In less than no time/
In a fleeting moment/

You're in the nooks and crannies/
Of the global melting-pot/
I make you climb/
The highest mountain in a split second/
I am a window on the world/
A new world of adventures/
I make you travel a myriad miles in a minute/
Seeing a thousand sights at a glance/
I let you dream a million dreams/
In the twinkling of an eye/
Broadening your horizons/
I nourish green minds/
Hia! Hia!/
Come good, Nouvelle Donne!/
The dawn of a New Deal/
Hia! Hia! /
The reign of meritocracy/
Hia! Hia! /
The demise of jungle justice/
Hia! Hia! /
The requiem for nepotism/
Hia! Hia! /
The death of cronyism/
Hia! Hia!/
The entombment of tribalism/
Hia! Hia!/
The cremation of chopbroke-*potism*[70]/
Hia! Hia!/
The cremation of shenanigans/
Hia! Hia! /
The burial of shady deals/

---

[70] Leading a hand-to-mouth life

Of scratch-my-back/
I-scratch-your-own credo/
Modus operandi of the city rank and file/
THE CITY…
Love or hate Ogoli/
Medley of beggars/muggers/ picketers/
The bulk of them varsity graduates/
On the payroll of the Street Community/
Jo'burg… City of Gold/
Crime capital of the world! /
Africa in miniature/
Habitat for the wretched of the earth/
Crammed in match-box shacks/
Slumbering and sniffing glue/
Dazed with hard drugs/
Under bridges/
In card boxes/
In shanty towns/
HILLBROW… Johannesburg/
Welcome to Our Hillbrow! /
Metonym for lawlessness /
Carnal merchandise! /
Ogoli—City of Gold/
Fallen from grace to grass/
Hub of thugs/The Underworld/
Of hard drug peddlers/
Brothel of carnal traders/
Gone haywire/
Gone are the days/
When Jo'burg was the heartbeat
Of Azanian Economy/
In this day and age/
Grime and crime are the hallmarks/

Of this dungeon/
Nay of this Golgotha/
Men of the underworld call the shots/
Drug lords duck and dive amidst gunshots/
Armed robbers mug and strangle with impunity/
In collusion with conmen from other climes/
Jo'burg
Rendez-vous for *feymen*[71]
Rallying at gunpoint in broad daylight/
Child whores vie ferociously/
With haggard old-timers for scarce clientele/
Jo'burg
Epithet for Mega tomb/
Hillbrow
Euphemistic hellhole/
I write what I want/
Because the pen/
Is mightier than the sword/
I write for prima donnas/
B...Fassie
Temperamental pop songster/
Madonna of the townships/
Wild child of Azanian pop music/
Big fry who gave voice/
To marginalized people of color/
No nonsense *tête brûlée*[72]
Who sent folks to dance floor/
Dancing out of breath nonstop/
The Color Bar in Soweto/
In Soshanguve/

---

[71] Conmen
[72] Hot headed person

Township in Azania/
In Cape Town/
In Durban/
In Limpopo/
In Tzaneen/
In Venda/
In Tzaneen/
A la manière de Queen/
Yvonne Chaka Chaka/
Princess of Dobsonville /
Who heartily sang: /
I'm burning up/
I cry for freedom/
Makoti/Motherland/
Umqombothi/Sangoma/
Be proud to be African/
Thank you Mr. DJ/
Back on my feet/
Rhythm of life/
Who does have the firepower? /
Bombani/
Tiko Rahini/
Kwenzenjani/
Alternatively, Mzwakhe Mbuli? /
Of Sophia town/
Poet of the People/
Indomitable gadfly/
Poète de renom/
Mbulism aka nightmare of /
The thieving Oligarchy/
In Union Buildings/
Power of Africa/
Hic! Hic! Huc! /

Hiccups of mental/
Masturbation and prevarication/
Hic! Hic! Huc! /
Hiccups of linguistic Glottophagia/
Hic! Hic! Huc! /
Hiccups of cultural Bastardization/
Hic! Hic! Huc!/
Hiccups of economic Asphyxiation/
Hic! Hic! Huc! /
Hiccups of the Rape
Of Mother Africa/
Hic! Hic! Huc!
Hiccups of Genocides/
Hic! Hic! Huc! /
Hiccups of Denigration/
In all shapes and colors/
Hic! Hic! Huc! /
Hiccups of graft, /
And kleptomania/
AND of wanton embezzlement/
Hic! Hic! Huc!
Hiccups of kickbacks/
AND of misappropriation/
Of public funds/
Hic! Hic! Huc!
And of collusion /
Hic! Hic! Huc! /
Hiccups of the vicious
Cycle of poverty and Dysphoria/
And of chronic Underdevelopment/
Hic! Hic! Huc! /
Phantoms of Apartheid/
And of the Boer War/

Waterloo of the English! /
Hic! Hic! Huc! /
Hiccups of endemic Misgovernment/
Hic! Hic! Huc! /
Hiccups of the fleecing /
Of Africa's natural resources/
Hic! Hic! Huc! /
Hiccups of the Balkanization/
Factions! Factions everywhere! /
Within the Ambazonian Revolution/
Constitutes our own very Undoing/
Southern Cameroons Defense Forces (SOCADEF)/
Headed by Ebenezer Akwanga/
Factions! Factions!
Hither and thither! /
To what end? /
Defense Sanitization Program (DSP)/
Headed by Lucas Cho Ayaba/
Factions! Factions! /
North, South, East and West/
What for? /
MoRISC, contraption concocted/
By Ntongfuon Boh Herbert/
Bona fide Ambazonian/
Corrupted overnight by Mammon/
Albatross or Bird of good omen? /
Raison d'être of this white elephant?
Answering is blowing in the wind/
Factions! Factions!
Right, Left and Center/
Pour quel but? /
South Cameroons National Council/
Another hydra headed by Elvis Kometa/

Or is it Vyvian Mbanwi/
Go tell is on the Mountain! /
Factions! Factions!
Ambazonia Defense Force (ADF)/
Bona fide grouplet/
Or one more green snake in green grass/
We are led by peacocks/
With heads full of shit/
And tails as long as Lake Oku/
Samuel Ikome Sako/
Alias-Fake Doctor! /
Church Mafioso/
Christopher Anu/
Amba Judas Iscariot/
Foul-mouthed punk/
Masquerading as Good Samaritan/
Lucas Cho Ayaba,
Another bogus Ph.D.!
Doctor without Dissertation (DWD)! /
Self-centered individual/
Drunken with power! /
They are legion/
All graduates of the University
Of Bonamoussadi in LRC!/
Where is Christmas Ebini
In this entire imbroglio? /
Is he a DWD too? /
Peu importe! /
What is his role in this Revolution? /
Gendarme of the Revolution?
Alternatively, settler of scores? /
That is the question! /
Where does Sisiku Julius Ayuk Tabe,/

Kondengui inmate feature/
In this Shopping Mall of Amba politics?
And Wilfred Tassang? /
What is his role in this
Cabal of dissidents? /
Why did Dabney Yerima decamp? /
Graft? Disillusion or Anomy? /
That is the question! /
Who is Christopher Fomunyoh?
Saboteur or Grise for Amba Sovereignty?
That is the question!/
Factions! Factors! /
Is this Nera Ten debacle/
A flea in my ear/
Or veritable bugbear? /
Who are these fellas? /
Messiahs or Anti-Christs? /
Who's paying these pipers/
In addition, who is calling the tune? /
These are not idle interrogations! /
Are we bona fide liberators/
Or wolves in Sheep's skin? /
That is the question! /
Are they Anti-Christs or messiahs? /
That is the question! /
Be not be fooled/
Our progeny is watching us/
Before long we will be summoned
By the tribunal of Retribution/
To each an account of our roles/
In the Ambazonian Revolution/
We'll take to the stand/
To give an Account of our roles

We did or did not do in/
This Liberation Struggle/
On that day, there will be
Weeping and gnashing of teeth.
Make no mistake about it! /
Woe to this clan of oppressors! /
They heed no law/
They're vultures/
They accept no correction/
Trust no one in the Struggle/
They are Islands sufficient
Onto themselves in/
Season and out of season/
Amba officials are roaring lions/
They are evening wolves/
Fickle chameleons! /
Its pastors are arrogant rogues/
They are treacherous men and women/
With no compunction about/
Acting against the grain in all they do/
Our priests are charlatans and conmen/
They do violence to the Revolution/
Some are emasculators of social anomy/
Feeding on the sweat and flesh of Amba boys/
Hibernating in the trenches of GZ! /
Woe betide kingmakers/
For theirs shall be days of agony/
Their wealth will be plundered/
Their homes demolished/
They'll build mansions with their loot/
But will not live in them/
They will plant vineyards/
But will not drink the wine/

It shall be worse than Sodom and Gomorrah! /
Nation of vampires/
Nation of vultures/
Nation of hyenas/
Nation of two-headed snakes/
Counterfeit nation in Africa!
iAfrica! /
Nkosi sikelel' iAfrika[73]/
God bless Africa/
Proscribe wars and strife/
Hear our prayers/
Pay heed to our whispers/
Harken the voice of the dead/
Lend your ears often/
To the things said by the invisible/
Listen to the whispers yonder/
Lend your ears always/
To the whistling of the wind/
Hear the voices in the waters/
The sobbing in the bushes/
It's the voices of ancestors/
They're in the shade of trees/
In the shadow of living beings/
They're in the lightening/
In the dazzling sunshine of the day /
In the pitch darkness of the night/
The dead are not dead/
We pray for Amba school kids/
Murdered by LRC vampires in Kumba/
We pray for the departed souls in Guzang/

---

[73] Title of the South African national anthem, composed by Enoch
Sontonga.

We pray for the departed souls in Batibo/
We pray for all fallen soldiers on GZ/
Whose blood watered the/
Ambazonian Tree of Liberty! /
They're in the quivering trees/
In the moaning plants/
They're in the running streams/
In the stagnant lakes/
They're in the creeks/
The dead are not dead[74]/
They're in the marketplaces/
They're in the dancing circles/
They're in the crowds/
They're not dead/
Listen to the hissing voices yonder/
They're the breath of ancestors/
They're not gone/
They're not in the grave/
The dead are never dead/
Listen to the voices of the dead/
In the breast of the nursing Mother/
In the wailing of the lone Child/
The dead are not dead/
They're in the dry grass/
They're not under the soil/
They're in the embers/
In the dry season fire/
In the dew of the Grassfields /
Of our Ambaland/
They're in the groaning rocks/

---

[74] Calqued on Birago Diop's poem titled "Souffles" published in his anthology Leurres et Lueurs, 2nd edition, by Présence Africaine, 1967.

In the grinning evergreen forests/
They're in the huts decimated by BIR/
They're in our demolished homes/
The dead are not dead.
Join the dead in chanting/
Hail! Hail! This Land of Glory[75]/
We the Ambazonians pledge our loyalty/
Praise the Son our Savior/
Who granted us the freedom/
Allegiance to the heroes who/
Bore the land with their blood/
Glory to Glory, we rise and never to fall/
Here in our nation flowing with milk and honey/
Glory, glory to the father, /
For making you a nation/
A joy forever more/
Ambazonia! Land of freedom, /
You shall live in plenty meeting our needs/
And your children shall be like the stars above/
The most high God be the watchman of this nation/
From the deep seas/
And over our mountains/
Ambas sing *Ambazonia! Land of freedom,/*
They sing Nkosi sikelel iAfrika!
Brain child of Enoch Sontonga/
Die Stem[76]/
Die stem van Afrika[77]
The clarion Call for African Unity/
Nkosi sikelel' iAfrika/

---

[75] Ambazonian National Anthem
[76] Afrikaans translation of the title of South Africa's national anthem.
[77] God bless Africa in Afrikaans

Setjhaba Darfur/
Lord bless Rwanda/
God bless Africa…
Woe onto those who
Mistake good for evil/
Woe onto those who
Confuse darkness with light/
Woe onto those who/
Taste bitter for sweet/
Woe onto those who
Who take mirage/
For reality/
So says my Teacher/
TEACHER…
Oh teacher! /
My dear teacher/
Sweet as honey/
Bright like the sun/
My loving teacher/
Your presence in class/
Keeps me awake…/
Oh my beloved teacher!
You move hither and/
Thither in the classroom/
Dressed to the nines/
Like an African princess/
Inculcating in us/
The pursuit of happiness/
HAPPINESS…
The first day I set my foot
In the white man's school/
Ma papa said to me:/
Son you shall never quit!

Quitters are losers/
The first day I set my eyes
On the white man's book/
My mama said to me:/
Son you dare not leave! /
A man without book in his head, /
Is like a house without occupants/
The first day I passed /
The white man's test/
My papa and my mama said to me:/
Son this is only the beginning/
Of big things to come/
The sky is the limit! /
When one says yes/
His *nyi* [78]says YES too/
When one says NO/
His *nyi*[79] says NO too/
Where there is a will,
There's always a way/
The first day I graduated/
From the white man's school/
My papa and my mama said to me:/
Son you are now a new man/
A man with balls between his legs/
You can now own a hut/
And take a wife if it pleases you/
You have done us proud! /
If *Fongombombi*[80] called us this day/
We'll hold our heads high/

---

[78] Guardian spirit
[79] Guardian spirit
[80] God –the –Great

And say to Him, /
Father here we are! /
All this thanks to my Teacher/
Oh my priceless teacher!
What will I be without you? /
I hope I shall one day be like you/
You don't give me a fish/
You teach me how to CATCH a fish/
My dear teacher/
What a blessing you are to me! /
Your ideas are invaluable/
Your outfit is my dress code/
Your words are my gospel/
Wow! My dear teacher! /
What a role model! /
You show me how/
To clean my dirty linen in private…
DIRT…DIRT… DIRT
Dirt in Mbalmayo/
Dirt in Kribi/
Dirt in Dibombari/
DIRT…DIRT… DIRT everywhere
Dirt in Bonamoussadi/
Dirt in Souza/
Dirt in Mokolo/
DIRT…DIRT… DIRT/
In all nooks and crannies/
Heaps of Dirt in Yaoundé/
Heaps of Dirt in Douala/
DIRT…DIRT… DIRT/
Dirt in offices/
Dirt in churches/
Dirt in schools/

DIRT...DIRT... DIRT/
Our National Commodity/
Heaps of Dirt in Maroua/
Heaps of Dirt in Garoua/
Heaps of Dirt in Ngoundéré
DIRT...DIRT... DIRT/
Dirt in njangi houses/
Dirt in palaces/
Dirt in Kwifon houses/
DIRT...DIRT... DIRT/
Genocidal dirt in Darfur/
Genocidal dirt in Rwanda—/
Slaughtering of Hutu by Tutsi/
And of Tutsi by Hutu/
Dirt on the face of Africa/
Indelible dirt on Mother Africa/
Vendetta for blood diamonds/
In Liberia and Sierra Leone/
Stain on the garment of Mama Africa/
Scuffle between the soldiers/
Of Nigeria and Cameroon/
For the sake of Bakassi/
Is dirt on Africa/
Child trafficking is a smut/
On the underpants of Africa/
Child enslavement is filth/
On the skin of Africa/

DIRT...DIRT... DIRT everywhere /
Proliferation of child soldiers
On the African continent/
Africa's sore finger/
Female genital mutilation/

Thorn in the FLESH of Africa/
Breast ironing is a shame on Africa/
I mean it is soot on the face of Africa/
Virginity testing alias *Umhlanga*[81]
Disgrace for Africa/
Widow inheritance is dirt on Africa/
Abduction/ rape/maiming/
Slaughtering of unarmed civilians/
In Northern Uganda by Joseph Kony's
Lord's Resistance Army/
Is sleaze on the beauty of Africa/
Boko Haram/
Government sponsored Islamic fanaticism/
Is dirt on mother Africa/
Harakat al-Shabaab is dirt on Africa/
Abdullah Azzam Brigades/
Is dirt on Africa/
Al- Mulathaneen/
Is dirt on Africa/
Al- Qaeda in Islamic Maghreb/
Is dirt on Africa/
Ansar-al Sharia in Libya/
Is dirt on Africa/
Ansar al- Sharia in Tunisia/
Is dirt on Africa/
Ansar Bait al-Maqdis/
Is dirt on Africa/
H-u-r-u-j-e!
Dawn of the/
UNITED STATES OF AFRICA!
H-u-r-u-j-e!

---

[81] Ritual reed dance

Muammar al-Gaddafi/
H-u-r-u-j-e!
The foot soldier of Africa/
H-u-r-u-j-e!
Warrior against Afro-pessimism/
H-u-r-u-j-e!
Combatant against battered self-image/
H-u-r-u-j-e!
Commander of Africa's Salvation Army/
H-u-r-u-j-e!
Hail Thomas Sankara/
That terrific guy from Upper Volta/
H-u-r-u-j-e!
Hail Patrice Lumumba/
That gladfly killed by lackeys/
Of the West in King/
Leopold's ghost land/
H-u-r-u-j-e!
Hail Rueben Um Nyobe/
Enfant terrible of Gaullist Africa[82]
That terrible guy from Cameroun/
Africa must unite or perish /
It boggles the mind /
To think that we will/
Salvage this continent by
Balkanizing it into ethnic concaves/
Into tribal fiefs and war zones/
This sort of tinkering spells doom/
The future of Africa/
Rests on our collective wisdom/

---

[82] Reference to Joseph Richard's book, Gaullist Africa: Cameroon Under Ahmadou Ahidjo (1992)

We cannot but unite/
Behind one banner/
To address our collective mishaps/
African intelligentsia/
Welcome a-board!
Gird your loins/
H-u-r-u-j-e!/
Sing Kum-Kum Massa!/
Oh! Kum-Kum! /
H-u-r-u-j-e!/
African youth/
Oh! Kum-Kum!
The turn is yours/
Oh! Kum-Kum! /
H-u-r-u-j-e!/
African women/
Oh! Kum-Kum!
Big, big *ngondere*[83]/
Oh! Kum-Kum! /
Small, small *ngondere*[84]/
Oh! Kum-Kum!
All hands on deck/
Oh! Kum-Kum! /
One time! GO! Africa! GO!/
Pick up the flickering torch/
Of Pan-Africanism/
NO TURNING BACK!
United we stand/
Divided we fall/
The onus is ours/

---

[83] Mature women
[84] Teenage girls

To rescue Africa/
Rescue Africa/ From re-colonization/
From neo-colonization/
From collective auctioneering/
Africa…
Not a continent for the taking/
Not China's New Colony/
Africa…
Not the Next Factor of the World/
Africa…
Not the lost continent/
Africa…
Not the Dark Continent/
Africa…
Not the Next Factory of the World/
Africa…
Not a tabula rasa/
Africa…
Not the continent that self-destroys/
Not a clean slate/
Africa…
Has not reached/
The proverbial point-
Of-no-return /
Africa…
Is not irredeemable/
Afro-pessimists/
Despoilers of our backyard/
May say what they want/
They're like mosquitoes/
MOSQUITO…
Nwing! Nwing!
Nocturnal songster/

Nwing! Nwing! /
Solitary chorister/
Nwing! Nwing!/
Avaricious bloodsucker/
Nwing! Nwing!
Ubiquitous sleep snatcher/
Nwing! Nwing! /
Creature so invisible/
And yet so visible/
Nwing! Nwing! /
MOSQUITO…
Friend or foe/
Of the human ear? /
Nwing! Nwing! /
Vector of human fear/
Nwing! Nwing! /
Conduit for malaria/
Nwing! Nwing!
Harbinger of insomnia/
Nwing! Nwing!
Insect so taciturn/
Yet so loquacious/
Nwing! Nwing! /
MOSQUITO…
He that loathes the mosquito/
Undoubtedly loves slumber/
Nwing! Nwing!
Mosquito/
Persona non grata/
In slumber land/
Nwing! Nwing! /
WE…
Disinfectants of illusions/

Soured/malignant/ crabbed/warped/
Fumigators of prejudice/
Color-bar monster/
Jim Crow/
Hendrik Frensch Verwoerd/
Architect of apartheid/
Race-cleansing spokesman/
Devil's advocate/
Sanctimonious hypocrite/
In thy mouth lies a fiery tongue/
Your lingo is hate: /
Kaffir! Coolie! Nigger! /
Epitome of bigotry and umbrage/
Is your God Lucifer? /
Black is anathema/
In thy hateful eyes/
Fawning blasphemer! /
The credo you worship: /
Racial segregation/
Yet you're no master /
Of your own libido/
Fornicating with colored mothers/
Having coitus with black sisters/
Pathological liar! /
Bow thy head in shame/
Your die is cast/days numbered/
Spent force/ your requiem sings/
Now you are a spent force/ adieu!
Thy house is split/
Populace be not fooled/
It's a misnomer/
Presidential palace/
Metaphor for impunity and abuse/

Beneath the glamour and glitter/
Lurks many a machination/
Survival of the fittest/
There goes the modus vivendi!
Here comes the ghost of/
 Jean-Irène/erstwhile First Lady/
Her ghost not laid to rest yet?
Hands dripping with blood/
Unashamedly, /
A call-girl steps into her sullied shoes/
To share the booty in the Shithouse/
Terrible disrepute for/
A nation in decrepitude! /
Stinks incest/
Reeks philandering/
We're skunks/
We exude perversion/
Tenants of the Etoudi/
Shithouse are vampires/
Here comes phantoms/
Of opponents fed to crocodiles/
In the Sanaga Maritime River/
S.O.S…/
There's fire in the house/
Run! Run! Run!
There is a storm in the palm-wine cup! /
Run! Run! Run! /
Le dehors est mauvais[85]/
Up kontri done wuo-wuo[86]/
Run! Run! Run! /

---

[85] Times do not bode well
[86] Things are topsy-turvy

There's hop-eye everywhere[87] /
Run! Run! Run! /
There's kelen kelen outside[88] /
Run! Run! Run! /
A sinister wind blows /
Run! Run! Run! /
Pandora's Box is open! /
Run! Run! Run! /
We call for a Sovereign /
National Conference /
Je dis Sans Objet[89]! /
We call for a Truth and /
Reconciliation Commission /
I say No way! /
Perpetrators squirming /
Victims fuming /
Who masterminded /
Who masterminded the chaos? /
Who orchestrated black-on-black violence /
Xenophobia or fight for economic survival? /
That is the question! /
Who bombed Khotso House? /
Who set fire on Magoo's bar in Durban? /
Who bombed Church Street? /
You planted landmines /
In Eastern Transvaal! /
Who is the arsonist of /
Amanzimtoti Shopping Center in Pretoria? /

---

[87] The act of opening one's eyes, which means the "act of intimidating or making people fear"

[88] It's slippery outside, which means the atmosphere is rife with uncertainty

[89] No way!

67

Speak up comrades! /
Time is running out! /
Who bears the brunt /
Of these calamities?
Umkhonto we Sizwe? /
Spear of the Nation? /
The Third Force? /
Self-Defense Units? /
Maybe Apla? /
Who? /
Remember: /
The Winnie United Football Club/
Mama's brainchild? /
You remember /
The State Security Council? /
Comrades, /
The day of reckoning/
Is around the corner/
The rank and file/
Demand the truth and nothing/
But the truth…oooh!/
Harken the war-chant: /
The tree of liberty is watered/
With the blood of martyrs! /
The price of liberty is /
Perpetual vigilance! /
The liberators of yesterday/
May well become the/
Oppressors of tomorrow! /
SIMUYE! /
We are one! /
Many tongues/
Different nations/

SIMUYE! /
One nation, one people/
Nations within a Nation/
Fiefs within fiefdoms/
From the ashes of apartheid/
Sprouts a New Nation/
The Nation of Rainbow colors/
Sing a lullaby/
Toyi! Toyi[90]!
Takes two to tango/
BUT…
A throng to *toyi-toyi*. /
Chant *toyi toyi* for fortification! /
Sing to glorify/
The fallen hero/
Of Umtata
Kingdom of King/
Sabata Dalindyebo/
Chant *toyi toyi*/
Sing to glorify/
The Fallen heroes of/
Sharpeville and Soweto/
Sing *toyi! toyi!*
To the unsung heroines/
of Soweto Uprising/
Sing *toyi! toyi!* /
To the death of Pass Laws/
And to the demise of/
Group Areas Acts/
Sing *toyi! toyi!* /
For the abrogation of Bantu Education/

---

[90] Protest march in South Africa in the era of Apartheid

Justice delayed/
Is tantamount to justice denied/
Heed this warning! /
Terminal imbecile! /
Chant toyi*! toyi!*
Sing to Soshanguve/
Hybrid nomenclature/
Chant toyi*! toyi!*
Sing in Fanagalo/
Sing in Sepedi/
Sing in Xhosa/
Chant toyi*! toyi!*
Sing in Setswana/
Sing in Tsotsitaal/
Township lingo/
Emblem of pacific cohabitation/
I walk tall/
Very tall/
Letting no hoodlum attempt to cow/
Me into submission/
Secure in my rugged persona/
Brooding no intimidation/
Unfazed by threats on my checkered life/
Let my diminutive statue/
Be not mistaken for frailty/
I am neither ostrich nor peacock/
I brave a myriad tribulations/
Not burying my head/
In phantasmagorical fine sand/
A la manière de Ostrich[91]/
Hip! Hip! Hooray!/

---

[91] Like

I am not a social chameleon/
Varying my pigmentation to tally with events/
That is why I sing UBUNTU! /
I am because you!
Hip! Hip! Hooray!
I am no hoax-box
Laughing up my sleeve/
In mock glee at human flaws/
I feel so I am/
Hip! Hip! Hooray!
I am no arbiter of divine designs/
Offspring of universal symbiosis /
UBUNTU my credo/
Hip! Hip! Hooray! /
Hymn to inmates/
Of global dungeons/
The world's a donjon/
Where the pious/
Cohabitate with the miscreant/
This asteroid is screwed up/
Doomed! Damned!
I wanna say what I gotta say/
No punk's gonna
Tell me to shut up!
I'm gonna write what I want/
No sissi's gonna tell me what to write/
I'm gonna say what I want/
No motherfucker's gonna /
Tell me what to write/
Dumbasses/ Jackasses! /
This underworld's sick/
Totally fucked up! /
In deep shit/Quagmire/Mire!

Gives me the creeps/
This joint's gone bonkers/
They now speak in tongues! /
These antichrists! /
Dirtballs/ hoodlums/scallywags/
Riff-raff/ nitwits/ thingamabobs/
At every nook and cranny/
Taking hostage the land of the free/
Ambazonia---/
Land of the great/ No Man's Land/
Darn assholes/cocky self-servers/
A jilted lover storms into/
A girl's apartment/
And pulls the trigger/
Poom! Poom! Poom!
Victim drops dead in a pool of blood/
Pandemonium!
A cuckolded husband/
Bursts into a love nest/
Armed to the teeth/
Swings a machete/
Hither and thither/
Gwag! Gwag! Gwag!
Wife and carnal thief drop dead/
Scandal! Consternation!
High school-kid flunks her test/
On account of binge-drinking/
And unbridled fornication/
Takes entire faculty hostage/
Fires fatal shots /
Pam! Pam!
Heads roll in hot blood!
Holy shit! / Bitch! /

Sauve-qui-peut général![92]

Does that solve the problem?

Maybe or maybe not/

Gun mania/

Our New credo/

I flex my muscles/

I prime my gun/

And pull the trigger/

Bang! Bang!

Foe drops down/

In a lake of cold blood/

Does that resolve the issue? /

Humankind is deranged!

Sick, indeed! /

I hear the voice of reason/

I hear it in the wilderness/

Crying for peace/ for pacification of souls/

Decrying bravado in futility/

Those are the voices of POWs/

Many tenants of …

GUANTANAMO…

Inhabitants of /

Kirikiri Maximum Security Prison/

Hide-out and dunghole/

Our Nemesis—/

History will judge us harshly/

For creating Guantanamo the world over/

Notorious prisons/

Home to prisoners of conscience/

From Far and near/

Robbed of inalienable rights/

---

[92] General stampede

Held captive/
In the middle of nowhere/
Symbol of legal limbo/
Sing requiem for Habeas Corpus/
Kookuututu! Kookuututu!
Kookaatata! Kookaatata!
Judicial aberration/
Kookuututu! Kookuututu!
Kookaatata! Kookaatata!
Playing accused and accuser/
Judge and defendant/
At the same time/
Miscarriage of Justice! /
There's rape in these precincts/
GREEN RAPE…/
On Earth Day/
Year in year out/
We pay lip service/
To environmental stewardship/
The worst despoilers make
The loudest noise. /
Yet…/
Our Clean Air Act/
Remains a loud-sounding nothing/
Not worthier than the sheet
On which it's written/
Our Clean Water Act a sham/
Pollution continues unabated/
We have turned our backs on
The Kyoto Protocol/
We've pulled out of the Paris Accord/
And stalled research
On renewable energy/

Green washing, /
Credo of our dirt-laden industries/
Human beings/
And nature/
Are on a collision course, /
Man's activities inflict/
Irreparable harm on Mother Earth/
Earth's endangered species/
A-plenty near extinction/
It's mind-boggling/
Four-legged animals are endowed/
With more wisdom than humans! /
There are great words/
In the animal kingdom /
One of such words is "Thanks"/
There are awesome words/
In animal lingo/
Two of such words are "Forgive me"/
There are awe-inspiring words/
In animal tongue/
Three of such words are "I love you"/
One wonders if human beings/
Will ever learn to think and speak /
Like animal beings/
Sometimes it feels like/
The life of humans is but a paradox/
We have very tall buildings/
But very short tempers/
We have extremely broad freeways/
But terribly narrow viewpoints/
We spend more but earn less/
Buy more but enjoy less/
More degrees we've amassed/

But not a modicum of sense/
More savvy but less judgment/
More experts we have/
But a myriad problems unresolved /
Our possessions we have multiplied/
Yet less value we derive/
We talk too much/
And lie too often/
A living we've learnt to make /
But not to live our lives/
All the way to the moon we have been/
But have trouble crossing the street/
To say howdy to our neighbors/
Outer space we've conquered/
But not inner space/
The atom we've split/
But not our prejudices/
We read too often but learn too little/
We've learned to rush but not to wait/
More haste less speed/
Higher incomes we have/
But lower morals/
More acquaintances/
But fewer friends/
These are the days of huge incomes/
But bigger debts/
Of glamorous weddings/
But more divorces/
These are the times of fancier houses/
But broken homes/
That's because Man lives/
In cobwebs/
A cobweb/

Is a network/
Of threads spun/
By a spider/
From secreted liquid/
It's a trap/
A REAL booby-trap/
For unsuspecting insects of prey/
An insidious entanglement/
For unwary human beings/
Our world is locked/
In a multitude of cobwebs/
Caught we are/
In our own web of intrigues.
Nonetheless…/
I have a dream that one day/
This asteroid will bounce /
Back to sanity/
On that day/
Ambazonia will know peace/
I have a dream…/
The blows have been hard
On Ambazonians/
They have pulled the punches/
To no avail/
But if God is with Ambazonians,
Who can be against them? /
I have a dream…/
The strife may be long/
But Ambazonians will/
Stay the course/
There's light at the end of the tunnel/
The times may be tough/
Ambazonians have held onto/

God's plans for the downtrodden/
They are not plans for disaster/
I have a dream…/
That one day Ambazonia/
Will be free…free at last! /
I shed tears for Ambazonia/
You know why Father, Lord/
Tears of muteness/
Words are buried under pain/
Frustration/
Sorrow/
Despondency/
Angst/
Melancholy/
Trauma/
Ambazonians are speechless/
Ambazonians are dumbfounded/
Ambazonians are crestfallen/
Ambazonians are flabbergasted/
But their tears you understand, O God/
Their wordless prayers/
You hear them, Lord/
Wipe away their tears, O God/
All their tears, Jesus/
Not tomorrow but today.

INDEX

Printed in the United States
by Baker & Taylor Publisher Services